Unlocking Financial Success

Understanding Class-Based Wealth Management

Table of Contents

Chapter 1. Introduction

In this Special Report titled "Unlocking Financial Success: Understanding Class-Based Wealth Management," we demystify the vastly multifaceted world of financial planning across socioeconomic strata. From high-earning individuals looking for wealth management advice, to those living just around the median income levels seeking dependable financial planning strategies, we've got everyone's interests at heart. Rather than using perplexing technical jargon, we unravel complex principles with an easy-to-follow, relatable approach, filled with actionable insights. Have you ever wondered how grand wealth was amassed over generations or how middle-class families managed to save for comfortable retirements? Leap into our report to learn all this and much more, as we guide you to your personal financial success. This report not just enlightens, but empowers you in understanding the nuances of socio-economically tailored wealth management approaches. Come, dive into the ocean of personal finance knowledge, and unlock your unique path to financial success!

Chapter 2. Understanding Socio-Economic Classes and Wealth

In order to get a comprehensive understanding of the dynamics involved in the wealth management process across different socio-economic classes, we first need to understand what these socio-economic classes mean and how they influence the accumulation and management of wealth. The socio-economic class of an individual or a family is not just an indicator of their present financial state, but it underlines the philosophies, behaviors, patterns, approaches, and expectations that shape their financial decisions.

2.1. Defining Socio-Economic Classes

Essentially, socio-economic classes can be seen as hierarchal groups within a society that are distinguished by certain economic and social situations. The placement of an individual or family within these groups can be determined by a multitude of factors, including income, educational attainment, type of profession, and overall wealth. Generally, these hierarchies are divided into three: the upper class, the middle class, and the lower class.

The upper class, often referred to as the economic elite, constitutes a small percentage of the population but controls a significant portion of total wealth. The middle class, meanwhile, represents a considerable cross-section of society, serving as the economic backbone in many countries. Finally, the lower class, consisting of individuals that are economically disadvantaged, significantly relies on social safety nets.

Understanding these distinctions is crucial not just for deciding where we fall in the economic spectrum, but also for engaging with our financial planning strategies, investment decisions, and wealth management approaches.

2.2. Wealth Across Socio-Economic Classes

Wealth distribution varies vastly across different socio-economic classes. The upper class typically possesses significant wealth in the form of investments, real estate, and other tangible and intangible assets. The middle class, on the other hand, often have a mix of assets that may include a home, retirement savings, and some form of investment. Lower income classes, however, usually have less accumulated wealth and might heavily rely on their regular paychecks to meet their living expenses.

Understanding this wealth distribution also empowers us to identify potential avenues for financial growth and improving our own socio-economic standings.

2.3. Money Management Philosophies

The philosophies around money management differ across socio-economic classes. The wealthy often consult a team of advisors for managing, preserving, and growing their wealth. They consider their wealth to be a tool for creating more wealth and focus on investing in high-risk, high-return ventures.

The middle-class families predominantly concentrate on wealth accumulation for achieving stability and security. They usually prioritize saving for their childs' education, buying a home, and preparing for retirement.

Lower-income individuals, confronted by the harsh realities of daily survival, do not usually have the luxury to think long-term concerning their finance. Their focus is on meeting immediate needs and overcoming financial difficulties.

These distinctive attitudes towards money shape the financial behavior of various socio-economic classes, their receptiveness to financial advice, and steps taken towards wealth accumulation and management.

2.4. The Pragmatics of Wealth Management

Wealth management strategies widely differ across socio-economic classes. The strategy that works best for a particular class might not be effective for others. Upper-class individuals often engage in wealth management approaches that involve sophisticated money management strategies, including hedge funds, private equity investments, and structuring trusts and foundations.

For the middle class, wealth management tends to involve more traditional elements, such as saving, budgeting, investing in stocks and bonds, and retirement planning. Lower-income individuals might prioritize personal finance management, debt relief, and strategies to raise their income.

2.5. Roadmap to Progress

Despite the differences, there is a shared desire amongst everyone to improve their financial situation. The road to financial progress begins with understanding one's current socio-economic class, then creating a tailored financial plan that aligns with that understanding. Irrespective of the class individuals fall into, the fundamental elements of financial success – living below one's means, saving and investing wisely, understanding financial risks, and leveraging opportunities – remain constant.

In conclusion, getting to grips with our socio-economic class and the interplay it has with wealth accumulation and management is crucial towards unlocking our financial success. Through this awareness, we can identify our strengths, acknowledge our limitations, and chart a course towards a more prosperous financial future.

Chapter 3. Journey to Prosperity: Wealth Accumulation Stage

Every prosperous journey begins with a single step. Similarly, the journey to financial prosperity begins with the accumulation stage. This period forms the foundation of wealth creation. It is the time when you increase your income, invest smartly, manage your expenses, and start building your wealth.

3.1. Understanding Wealth Accumulation

As the name suggests, wealth accumulation refers to the phase where you start earning and retaining income. To understand this process better, it's essential to dive into the key elements that constitute wealth accumulation: income, savings, and investment.

1) Income

Income is the primary source of wealth accumulation for most of us. It can come from various sources such as a salaried job, self-employment, business, or freelancing. The goal is to keep increasing your income while keeping expenses in check.

2) Savings

Savings are the portion of your income that you don't spend. Every dollar saved is a dollar earned, so it's vital to cultivate the habit of saving right from the start. A savings strategy should include setting a budget, tracking expenses, and keeping a portion of your income aside regularly.

3) Investing

Investing is the key to multiply your savings. This could involve investing in stocks, bonds, real estate, or any other kind of asset that can increase in value or provide income.

3.2. Earning and Saving: The First Steps

To accumulate wealth, you must first earn an income and then save a portion of that income. It's crucial to remember that saving is not merely left-overs after spending; it is a commitment you make to your future self.

1) Earning:

Selecting a career path that drives your passion and pays you well is the first step of wealth accumulation. Aim to enhance your skills continually, allowing you to increase your income potential progressively. You can do this by acquiring new qualifications, learning on the job, attending workshops, or networking with industry veterans.

2) Saving:

The easiest way to save is to follow the 50/20/30 rule. This strategy suggests you divide your after-tax income, spending 50% on needs, 20% on savings, and 30% on wants. By following this rule, it becomes easier to manage and monitor your savings.

3.3. Investing Wisely

While saving provides a solid foundation, investing kickstarts the wealth multiplication process. Investing wisely means putting your money in various vehicles that have the potential to increase your wealth.

1) Diversify Investments:

A diversified investment portfolio helps to minimize risk and optimize returns. It involves spreading your investments across different asset classes like stocks, bonds, real estate, and cash equivalents.

2) Long-Term Investing:

Patience is cardinal when it comes to investing. Wealth accumulation is a long-term game where time is your best friend. The concept of compounding plays a significant role here: the longer you hold your investments, the more they are likely to grow.

3) Regular Investing:

Ensure to follow a disciplined approach to investing. Regularly investing a fixed amount can help you take advantage of market volatility, a concept known as Dollar-Cost Averaging (DCA). DCA allows you to buy more shares when prices are low and fewer shares when prices are high, which can result in a lower average cost per share over time.

3.4. Debt Management

Accumulation of wealth also involves steering clear of unmanageable debt. This involves focusing on good debt that creates value or produces income and avoiding bad debt that does not increase in value or generate income.

1) Leveraging Good Debt:

Good debt can be an investment that will grow in value or generate long-term income. For instance, student loans can lead to a better job and higher income in the future. Mortgages allow you to own real estate that may increase in value in the long run.

2) Avoiding Bad Debt:

Bad debt primarily includes things that rapidly depreciate in value and do not generate long-term income. An example is credit card debt, which often comes with a high-interest rate and funds consumable goods that depreciate over time.

3.5. Conclusion

Each phase of your life requires a different approach to money management and wealth accumulation. Understanding the processes involved, strategies to follow, and common pitfalls to avoid can greatly enhance your journey towards financial prosperity. Remember, wealth accumulation is a marathon, not a sprint. Patience, discipline, and consistent effort will guide you in unlocking financial success. Ultimately, the path to prosperity lies in striking a balance between income growth, intelligent saving, wise investing, and prudent debt management.

Chapter 4. The Middle Class Route: From Savings to Investments

Financial stability is a vital component of modern lives. Even more so for the middle class, which tends to comprise more than 50% of the society. In this section, we aim to explore financial strategies that enable the middle-class individual to grow wealth progressively. We'll delve deeply into savings, investments, the art of balancing between expenses and investments, and the much needed emergency fund.

4.1. Beginning With Savings

The cornerstone of financial success amongst middle-class individuals is a disciplined savings approach. Reserve a portion of your income to ensure you are consistently adding to your wealth. This might sound fairly simple, but it requires careful budget planning and meticulous tracking of your expenses.

Most financial advisors recommend a 50-30-20 rule when it comes to budget allocation, where 50% of the net income is dedicated to necessities, 30% to wants, and finally, 20% to savings and debt repayment. To facilitate easy tracking of expenses, leverage various digital tools and applications which can categorize transactions and uncover your spending patterns.

The goal here is to save consistently, even if the amount is small. Over time, with the power of compound interest, these savings can accumulate into a substantial fund. It's never too late to start saving, but the earlier you start, the better.

4.2. Moving Towards Investments

Once you've established a steady savings pattern, you can begin exploring investment opportunities. Investing is essential to counteract inflation and ensure the real value of your money doesn't diminish.

The middle-class population has a wide array of options to consider - stocks, bonds, mutual funds, real estate, and even newer vehicles like cryptocurrencies. Each one carries its pros and cons, as does the level of risk involved. Therefore, it's vital to understand your own financial goals, risk appetite, and time horizon before diving into investments.

Divide your investments into short-term, medium-term, and long-term based on your financial objectives. If you're saving for your child's college education in seven years, that's a medium-term goal. But planning for retirement that's 20 years away is a long-term goal. A vacation you're planning next year is a short-term goal. Different goals will require different investment strategies and vehicles.

4.3. Striking A Balance

The fine art of balancing between expenses, savings, and investments is pivotal to navigating the middle-class financial expedition. It requires a good understanding of your financial situation and disciplined money management skills.

While it might be tempting to invest heavily for quicker wealth accumulation, bear in mind that overcommitting can jeopardize your financial health in case of market downtrends. Likewise, overspending on wants may hamper your ability to save. The key is to maintain a healthy balance and adjust the allocations based on economic conditions, lifestyle changes, and financial goals.

4.4. Building An Emergency Fund

An often overlooked yet crucial aspect of financial planning is building an emergency fund. This savings buffer can cover unexpected expenses such as sudden medical emergencies, job loss, or any unforeseen event that disrupts your regular income.

Financial advisors often recommend that your emergency fund should ideally cover three to six months of your living expenses. The exact amount, however, will depend on your personal circumstances, job security, and risk tolerance.

4.5. Conclusion

A financial journey that begins with steady savings and culminates into strategic investments ensures a secured path towards financial success. It may seem overwhelming initially, but with time and discipline, navigating the world of finance will become a rewarding endeavor. Adopting these practices can empower you to leverage your middle-class status as a stepping stone towards financial growth and stability.

Chapter 5. Reaping Benefits: The Ins and Outs of Investment Dividends

Investing is an art and science combined - a calculated act of taking calculated risk now, for potential benefits in the future. The benefits, commonly known as returns on investment, are primarily twofold: capital gains and dividends. Capital gains represent an increase in the investment's value over time, whilst dividends signify a share of profits distributed by the company to its shareholders. This chapter shines a spotlight on the latter i.e., dividends, their dynamics, and strategies to exploit them optimally for wealth generation.

5.1. The DNA of Dividends

Dividends play a critical part in a company's life. They are usually remnants of a company's net income, decided by the board of directors, to be allocated and dispersed among its shareholders. Dividends can take various forms - cash, additional stocks, or other property. It's important to understand that the decision of whether or not to disburse dividends, and how much to distribute, rests with the company's board.

A significant aspect of dividends is the dividend yield. This metric shows the ratio of a company's annual dividend to its stock price. Higher dividend yields suggest greater returns on investment.

5.2. Dividend Dates Explained

Understanding dividend dates is crucial to strategizing your investments. Four key dates are essential - the declaration date, ex-dividend date, record date, and the payment date.

1. **Declaration Date**: This is when the company's board of directors declares that a dividend will be paid.

2. **Ex-Dividend Date**: If you purchase a stock on its ex-dividend date or after, you will not receive the dividend. The stock begins trading without the value of its next dividend payment from this date.

3. **Record Date**: This is the date on which the company reviews its records to decide exactly who its shareholders are. An investor must be listed as a holder of record to ensure the dividend payment.

4. **Payment Date**: This is the date when the dividends are actually deposited into the investor's account.

5.3. Tax Implications and Dividends

Dividends aren't a free lunch; like every income, these are subject to taxation. In the United States, for instance, dividends are categorized as either 'qualified' or 'non-qualified'. Qualified dividends benefit from a lower tax rate as they fulfill certain criteria set out by the IRS. It is critical to consult with a tax professional or financial advisor to understand the tax implications of your dividend income.

5.4. DRIPs: A Way to Reinvest Dividends

Dividend Reinvesting Plans (DRIPs) are offered by many companies and provide the opportunity to reinvest cash dividends into additional shares. This strategy plays on the concept of compounding, essentially enabling an investor's equity holdings and wealth to grow faster.

DRIPs are a perfect choice for investors who prefer to take a long-term view and are content to see their wealth grow incrementally over time. A potential downside, however, might be the constraint on liquid cash, as all dividends are automatically reinvested back into the stocks.

5.5. Dividend Aristocrats: The Kings of Consistency

Dividend Aristocrats represent an exclusive group of companies that have consistently paid and increased their dividends annually for at least 25 consecutive years. This reliability offers a degree of predictability and security for investors, and such companies tend to perform well over the long term. Investing in these Aristocrats can be a robust strategy for regular income while waiting for potential capital appreciation.

5.6. The Dividend Capture Strategy: A Short-Term Gambit

Not everyone waits years for dividend payoffs. The Dividend Capture Strategy is a more aggressive method that aims to profit from dividends in the short-term. The idea here is to own the stock just long enough to earn the dividends, and then sell it off. However, one might have to bear trade expenses and tax implications, which could offset the benefit. So, consider this strategy with due caution and consultation.

In conclusion, dividend investing offers a potentially stable path toward financial growth as it offers regular income and capital appreciation over time. However, the considerations are many - tax implications, reinvestment strategies, and deciding between long or short-term dividend earnings. The right knowledge and strategy can help maximize the gains from investments, making dividends a powerful tool in your financial toolkit.

Chapter 6. Defying Gravity: Strategies for the Wealthy to Grow Richer

As an embodiment of prosperity, the wealthy class has unique opportunities and challenges when it comes to wealth management. As financial resources multiply, the complexity of managing them also escalates, inviting the need for a strategic and structured approach towards maximizing returns and minimizing risks. Embrace the strategies that not only defy gravity but also elevate financial success to unimagined heights for the affluent.

6.1. The Pinnacle of Tax Optimization

A central issue in wealth management is effective tax planning. The wealthy pay more in absolute terms and are often subject to a maze of complex tax laws. Understanding these laws and their implications can unlock significant savings.

To approach tax planning optimally, consult experienced tax advisors for advice on specialized financial instruments, like Trusts, Foundations or Special Purpose Vehicles (SPV). They can help you navigate the tax landscape, incorporating the benefits of legal loopholes to reduce your taxable wealth.

Estate planning is another vital element in tax optimization. A comprehensive estate plan, including wills, trusts, and beneficiary designations, help manage estate taxes and safeguard your wealth for future generations.

6.2. The Power of Diversification

Another fundamental strategy is diversification. Not keeping all the eggs in one basket is a simple yet effective strategy for achieving stable returns.

For the wealthy, diversification isn't limited to different sectors or geographies. It extends beyond traditional securities to alternative investment options like commercial real estate, venture capital, private equities, and even artwork or wines.

While alternative investments can deliver significantly higher returns than traditional assets, they also come with unique risks. Therefore, understanding the risk-return trade-off in these alternative assets is essential.

6.3. Real Estate: A Solid Foundation

Real estate has been a pillar of wealth creation for centuries. For wealthy individuals, real estate isn't merely a tangible asset; it's an opportunity to diversify and optimize returns.

Investing in commercial real estate can bring stable rental revenues and potential capital appreciation over time. In addition, real estate investment trusts (REITs) offer an easier route to invest in property without the need to manage it, spreading the risk across a portfolio of properties.

6.4. Private Equity and Venture Capital: The High-Risk, High-Return Game

Private equity and venture capital are high-risk, high-return investment opportunities. These investments require understanding of industries and businesses, a well-connected network to identify opportunities, and considerable time for due diligence.

Despite the intense effort required, these investments can potentially lead to exceptional returns when made wisely. However, bear in mind that private equity or venture capital investments should only represent a fraction of your total investment portfolio.

6.5. The Art of Philanthropy

Philanthropy isn't just about giving; it's also about strategic tax planning. Generous giving can lead to substantial tax deductions if appropriately managed.

By setting up a foundation or a charitable trust, the affluent can ensure their wealth not only contributes to social causes but also helps mitigate tax implications. However, these structures require diligent planning and ongoing management, so working with a specialized advisor is crucial.

6.6. Investments in Education: Planting Seeds for Future Generations

For wealthy families, focusing on the next generation's education is not just a responsibility but a long-term investment strategy. By cultivating the family's human capital, they significantly enhance their family's long-term wealth strategy.

Institutions like Ivy League universities can facilitate rich networks and opportunities that could help solidify a family's wealthy status in the future. Higher education is a worthy venture in someone's potential, which, in turn, can create a valuable return on investment.

6.7. The Role of Advisors and Wealth Managers

Despite possessing financial acuity, wealthy individuals can greatly benefit from the expertise of wealth managers. These professionals bring a holistic perspective, considering the interconnectedness of different components of an individual's wealth. Their advice is enriched with market insights, helping the wealthy maintain and grow their wealth.

In conclusion, wealth management for the affluent is not a singular task but requires a diversified, multi-generational, and inclusive approach. By leveraging the right mix of tax planning, investment diversification, philanthropy, and education investments, the wealthy can safeguard and multiply their wealth, creating a legacy that lasts beyond their own lifetimes. With the assistance of seasoned advisors, managing wealth becomes less of a challenge and more of an opportunity.

Chapter 7. The Role of Insurance in Wealth Preservation

Insurance has long been recognized as an essential tool for preserving wealth. It safeguards assets and financially provides for the future, mitigating risks that could erode hard-earned wealth.

7.1. Understanding the Fundamental Principles of Insurance

At its core, insurance is a contract ('policy') between the insurer and the policyholder. In this contract, the insurer agrees to pay for specific types of loss or damage borne by the policyholder in return for regular payments, known as 'premiums'. The principle behind insurance is 'risk transfer'. Essentially, the policyholder transfers their financial risk to the insurer who 'pools' the risk across numerous policyholders. This pooling permits the insurer to pay out claims as they arise, as the combined premiums fund these payments.

The two main types of insurance are life insurance and general insurance. While life insurance provides coverage on the policyholder's life, general insurance covers assets such as property, vehicles, health, etc.

7.2. The Relevance Of Insurance to Wealth Preservation

Insurance plays a pivotal role in financial planning as an effective wealth preservation tool. Here are a few ways how:

Protection Against Unforeseen Circumstances: Catastrophes can occur at any time, causing significant financial drain. Quality insurance plans minimize the financial consequences of these events and protect the wealth you've accumulated.

Estate Planning: Life insurance, for instance, can provide an inheritance or pay estate taxes, ensuring your wealth is smoothly transferred to the next generation.

Income Protection: If you're unable to earn income due to illness or injury, insurance can replace a portion of your income, securing your financial status.

7.3. Life Insurance: A Key Tool for Wealth Preservation and Transfer

Understanding life insurance as a means of wealth preservation requires focusing on various policy types.

Term Life Insurance: This straightforward policy covers you for a specific period ('term'). If you die during the term, the policy pays out a benefit to your named beneficiaries.

Whole Life Insurance: This policy covers you for your entire life and tends to be more expensive than term insurance. Importantly, it includes a cash value component that grows over time, providing a source of wealth that can be borrowed against or cashed in.

Universal Life Insurance: A more flexible approach to whole life insurance, allowing you to vary premiums and death benefits, and also has a cash value component.

With life insurance, wealth can be transferred to your heirs in a tax-efficient way and provide an immediate infusion of liquidity upon your death - both indispensable for wealth preservation.

7.4. General Insurance: Protecting Assets, Mitigate Risks

General insurance covers a variety of assets and situations, including vehicle insurance, health insurance, home insurance, travel insurance, and more. Each of these plays a crucial role in wealth preservation.

Home Insurance: This covers damage to your property and possessions, ensuring that you wouldn't need to spend significant sums for repairs or replacements after an unforeseen event.

Vehicle Insurance: This can pay for car repairs after an accident or replace your vehicle if stolen, thereby guarding against abrupt, large expenses.

Health Insurance: This mitigates the financial risks of illness and injury. Without it, a health crisis could rapidly deplete your wealth.

7.5. Conclusion: Insurance as a Cornerstone of Financial Planning

As we've seen, insurance plays an integral part in preserving wealth. Whether it's mitigating risks, providing for the future, or ensuring a smooth wealth transfer, your insurance policies are not just protective measures but strategic tools in the larger picture of financial planning. Therefore, it's crucial to deliberate insurance choices carefully, considering both present needs and future aspirations to maintain a secure economic path and unlock long-term financial success.

Chapter 8. Retirement Planning: A Must for Every Class

A robust retirement plan is not a luxury for the select few; it's a necessity for everyone, irrespective of one's socio-economic standing. It's the key to ensuring financial security and comfort in the twilight years of one's life. This chapter provides both a broad understanding of the importance of retirement planning and specific strategies for following up based on your socio-economic class.

8.1. Why Retirement Planning is a Must

The most crucial point to comprehend is that everyone will retire someday. Often people believe that they can work for life and thus ignore retirement planning, which is a grave mistake. With life expectancy on the rise, you could spend up to a third of your life in retirement, which requires adequate financial preparation.

Social Security or other similar public pension systems in many countries are barely enough to sustain a decent living standard, so being self-sufficient is the need of the hour. Rising healthcare costs, inflation, and an uncertain economic climate are all factors contributing to an increasingly challenging retirement scenario.

8.2. Basic Steps for Successful Retirement Planning

Effective retirement planning involves several key steps, regardless of your income level:

1. Understand Your Retirement Needs: As a general rule, you will
   need about 70-80% of your pre-retirement income to maintain
   your current standard of living once you stop working.

2. Start Saving and Keep Saving: It's never too early or late to start
   saving for retirement. The earlier you start, the more time your
   money has to grow.

3. Understand Your Retirement Plans: Be clear about your
   employer's retirement savings plan and make the most of it.
   Many companies match the amount that you contribute to these
   plans up to a certain limit.

4. Consider Basic Investment Principles: How you save can be as
   important as how much you save. Investments should be made
   based on your age and financial risk tolerance.

5. Don't Touch Your Retirement Savings: Try not touch your
   retirement savings, let them grow over time. If you withdraw
   from these accounts before you are supposed to, you may lose tax
   benefits or have to pay penalties.

8.3. Class-Based Retirement Plans

Different socioeconomic classes need tailored retirement planning
strategies because of differing monetary resources, goals, and
financial security layers.

8.3.1. Retirement Planning for Low-Income Individuals

Financial planning when resources are scarce requires attentiveness
and budgeting skills. Savings might be less, but there are ways to
kickstart the retirement planning process. Low-income individuals
should focus on:

1. Taking full advantage of employee-sponsored retirement plans,

especially if employers match contributions.

2. Utilizing savings vehicles like IRAs that offer potential tax advantages.

3. Automating a percentage of every paycheck to go directly into a retirement savings account.

4. Leveraging government programs like Social Security strategically and as soon as eligible.

8.3.2. Retirement Planning for Middle-Income Individuals

Understanding how to manage your money is essential for those in the middle-income bracket. Some concrete steps for planning retirement are:

1. Maximizing employer-sponsored retirement savings plans like 401(k)s or 403(b)s.

2. Also, investing in more diverse portfolios such as mutual funds, stocks, bonds, or real estate for additional income streams.

3. Exploring various tax-advantaged retirement savings options like traditional or Roth IRAs.

4. Engaging a financial planner if possible, to strategically plan out retirement savings goals and methods.

8.3.3. Retirement Planning for High-Income Individuals

High-income individuals typically have access to more monetary resources for retirement planning, but they also have unique challenges due to tax considerations and ensuring their wealth is preserved for future generations. Here are some pointers:

1. Utilizing tax-sheltered accounts and strategically planning

withdrawals to minimize taxation.

2. Creating diversified investment portfolios to spread out risk.

3. Engaging professional wealth managers for more complex financial planning needs.

4. Planning for estate taxes and considering wealth transfer strategies.

8.4. Adapt and Review Your Plan Regularly

The financial landscape changes, and with it, your retirement plan needs to evolve. Regular reviews and maintenance of your retirement plan are as important as setting it up in the first place. Make adjustments according to changes in income, expenses, or financial objectives.

Remember, retirement planning is no longer restricted to a particular socioeconomic class. It has become an integral part of financial planning for every individual across the spectrum. Act today to ensure your tomorrow is comfortable and secure.

Chapter 9. Taxation: Structuring Finances for Minimizing Liabilities

Managing finances is a daunting task, especially in the face of hefty taxes. One cannot deny the importance of taxation in keeping economies intact. However, with effective strategies and a comprehensive understanding of tax laws, individuals can structure their finances in ways that can potentially minimize tax liabilities. From understanding tax brackets, to leveraging tax-deferred investments, to mastering the art of tax deductions, this chapter illuminates the many aspects of structuring finances to minimize liabilities.

9.1. Understanding Tax Brackets

To thoroughly lay the groundwork for tax planning, understanding the basics of tax brackets is of paramount importance. Tax brackets are ranges of income to which different tax rates apply - the more you earn, the higher the tax rate. However, it's important to remember that progressing to a higher tax bracket doesn't mean that all your income will be taxed at that higher rate. Instead, each portion of your income within a certain range is taxed at its corresponding rate.

Consider, for instance, if you're an individual taxpayer in the U.S., your income is divided among seven tax brackets - 10%, 12%, 22%, 24%, 32%, 35%, and 37%. If your taxable income falls within the third bracket (22%), not all your income would be taxed at 22%. Only the income that falls within that bracket's range would be.

9.2. Using Tax-Deferred Investments

One of the key strategies to relieve the immediate burden of taxes is tax-deferred investing. A tax-deferred investment, as its name implies, is an investment in which certain tax effects occur at a future point in time, rather than in the period in which they actually occurred. Examples of tax-deferred accounts include Individual Retirement Accounts (IRAs), 401(k) plans, and annuities, among others.

Let's say you contribute to a traditional IRA or a 401(k). The money you put into these accounts is deducted from your income before taxes, hence lowering your total taxable income. The funds in these accounts then grow tax-free until withdrawal, which is usually at retirement when many people fall into a lower tax bracket.

9.3. Mastering Tax Deductions

Another way to reduce taxable income is through tax deductions, which are expenses that the government allows you to subtract from your taxable income. The more deductions you can claim, the less income you'll have reported, which in turn means you'll owe less in taxes.

Some deductions, like the standard deduction, are available to all taxpayers. For the tax year 2021, the standard deduction is $12,550 for individuals, $25,100 for married couples filing jointly, and $18,800 for heads of household.

You can also itemize deductions. Itemized deductions are expenditures listed on Schedule A of Form 1040 that you incurred throughout the year and can reduce your taxable income. These deductions include medical and dental expenses, state and local taxes, mortgage interest, and charitable contributions, among other expenditures.

However, it's important to note that you cannot claim both the standard deduction and itemize your deductions – you have to choose one or the other. It usually makes sense to use the one that allows for the largest reduction in taxable income.

9.4. Capital Gains Tax and Its Management

Capital gains tax is applied to the increase in value of a capital asset—like real estate, stocks, or bonds—when the asset is sold. The tax rate applied depends on how long you held the asset before selling it.

Short-term capital gains occur when an asset is sold within a year of acquisition and are taxed as ordinary income. Long-term capital gains, on the other hand, occur when an asset is held for more than a year before it's sold.

One strategy to manage capital gains tax is to hold onto assets for at least one year before selling. This allows the sale to be considered a long-term capital gain and to be taxed at a lower rate.

9.5. Making Most of Tax Credits

Unlike deductions, which reduce the amount of your income subject to tax, tax credits reduce your tax bill directly, dollar-for-dollar. There are two types of tax credits: refundable and non-refundable.

Refundable tax credits are those that can reduce your tax liability below zero and result in a refund. Non-refundable tax credits can reduce your liability to zero, but not beyond that point.

Examples of these tax credits include the Earned Income Tax Credit (EITC), the Child and Dependent Care Credit, and the American Opportunity Tax Credit. Understanding the various types of tax credits and their eligibility requirements can help ensure you're not missing out on valuable savings.

9.6. Estate Planning and Taxes

Lastly, a crucial part of structuring finances for minimizing liabilities lies within the realm of estate planning. Estate planning allows you to transfer your assets to beneficiaries in a tax-efficient manner through the use of tools like trusts and gifts.

A deep dive into the mechanisms of estate taxation and the toolbox of strategies commonly used to minimize its impact will be provided later in the chapter titled "Estate Planning: Transferring Wealth Across Generations."

Keeping in tune with the latest changes in the taxation system, forming a well-informed strategy according to your specific financial context, and consulting with a tax advisor can definitely make a difference in your tax bottom line, helping you unlock financial success. Remember, it's not just about how much money you make, but also about how much you get to keep after taxes.

Chapter 10. Estate Planning: Securing Wealth for Future Generations

Effective estate planning is amongst the key strategies that can ensure wealth preservation for future generations. It requires more than just writing a will. It involves a comprehensive approach which includes tax considerations, succession planning and asset protection. It's truly a remarkable way of securing financial wellbeing of future generations and ensuring your legacy.

10.1. Understanding Estate Planning

Estate planning is the process of determining how your wealth will be distributed to your heirs. The term "estate" refers to everything that you own – your financial accounts, real estate, personal possessions, and even your debts. By formulating a comprehensive estate plan, you're given the unique privilege to decide, in advance, who inherits your assets and how, when, and under what circumstances they access them. An effective estate plan can mitigate estate taxes, legal fees, and court costs, avoiding unnecessary financial loss.

10.2. Building a Solid Estate Plan

Here are some crucial steps involved in building a comprehensive estate plan:

1. Inventory Your Assets: Your estate plan will include anything of value that could be passed on to heirs. This includes properties, investments, business interests, retirement savings, insurance policies, intellectual property and personal possessions of value.

2. Understand Your Total Net Worth: It's vital you can articulate your financial situation clearly so that any legal or financial advisor can better assist in the planning process.

3. Identify Your Heirs: Determining what you want to happen to your assets when you're gone is an essential part of planning your estate. Take time to articulate who your beneficiaries are.

4. Establish a Will or Trust: A will is a legal document outlining how your property should be distributed upon death. A trust, however, functions during your lifetime and also stipulates asset distribution after death. We will talk more about these options later in this chapter.

5. Designate Legal Guardian: If you have minor children, it's critical to designate a guardian to care for them should something happen to you.

10.3. Elements of an Estate Plan

Key documents of an estate plan include:

1. Wills: This legal document lays out who will inherit what. It also allows you to name a guardian for your minor children and an executor who will carry out your wishes.

2. Trusts: Establishing a trust can reduce estate tax liability, avoid probate, and provide for minor children or family members who might be incapable of managing their finances. Trusts also provide for greater control of your wealth.

3. Power of Attorney: This document allows you to appoint someone to act on your behalf if you become incapacitated and cannot manage your own affairs.

4. Health care Proxy: Similar to power of attorney, a health care proxy is one who makes medical decisions on your behalf when you're unable to.

5. Beneficiary Designations: It's advisable to regularly review those you've designated as beneficiaries on your insurance policies, retirement accounts, and other assets.

10.4. Benefits of Proper Estate Planning

The benefits of estate planning go beyond wealth preservation. Here are some key reasons it's integral to financial planning:

1. Reducing Taxes: Estate planning can help minimize estate and inheritance taxes, leaving your heirs with more of your wealth.

2. Avoiding Probate: Probate can be a long, costly process. Estate planning can streamline the distribution of assets and bypass probate entirely.

3. Ensuring Family Care: Estate planning allows you to provide for loved ones, particularly those with special needs, both during your lifetime and afterward.

4. Maintaining Privacy: When an estate goes through probate, asset distribution becomes a matter of public record. A well-designed estate plan ensures your estate remains confidential.

10.5. Impact on Different Wealth Classes

High-income individuals may benefit from advanced tactics to mitigate estate tax exposure, while middle-income families may focus more on avoiding probate or creating trusts for the benefit of minor children or grandchildren.

Wealthy families should discuss charitable giving, family limited partnerships, and dynasty trusts as part of their estate plan. Families with modest wealth might avoid probate through the creation of revocable living trusts and ensuring beneficiary designations on key assets, like retirement accounts and life insurance policies, are updated.

Despite the aforementioned differences, the fundamental goals of maintaining family harmony, protecting the estate, and securing the future of the next generations remain common across all strata.

Estate planning is a huge part of a journey to financial success. As this chapter outlined, estate planning is vital at all economic levels. The methodology may vary, but the end game remains the same: to protect your loved ones, provide for them after your death, and build a legacy that can endure for generations.

Chapter 11. Financial Success: Creating Your Personal Path

There's no one-size-fits-all path to financial success; like our lives, each journey is unique. However, some time-tested principles can guide and steer you towards creating your tailored route to wealth accumulation and management.

11.1. Understanding the Definition of Success

Let's start with understanding your definition of success. It doesn't always need to mean being a billionaire or owning several properties. Often, financial success is about achieving financial freedom, which is different for each individual.

For some, it connotes having enough to cover monthly bills, occasional luxuries, and comfortably retire. For others, it means being able to afford a private education for their children or even to travel the world. Once you understand what financial success means to you, you are ready to set your goals.

11.2. Setting Financial Goals

The first step to achieving financial success is clearly defining your short, medium, and long-term goals. It's crucial to consider both your current and desired future lifestyle when forming these goals.

1. Short-term goals: These typically stretch up to a year and might include saving for a vacation, paying off a small debt, or even setting up an emergency fund.

2. Medium-term goals: These span from one to five years and might involve saving for a down payment on a home, starting a businesses, or obtaining a degree.

3. Long-term goals: Generally five years or longer, these usually revolve around retirement plans, paying off a mortgage, or achieving a significant net worth.

The key to setting robust and achievable goals is being realistic and keeping your plans flexible since life is often unpredictable.

11.3. Developing a Budget

One of the basic tenets of financial success is developing a budget and sticking to it. It is your roadmap, guiding you through your expenditures and helping you save.

1. Assess your income: Include all your sources of income, whether it's your salary, part-time job earnings, or income from rentals or investments.

2. Evaluate your expenses: Look at your spendings carefully, divide them into essential (like housing, food) and discretionary (leisure, hobbies) expenses.

3. Set your budget: After evaluating your income and expenditure, set a budget that leans more towards savings and investments.

4. Track your expenses: You're bound to fail if you don't monitor your expenses regularly.

There are many tools and apps that can help you keep your budget in check and track your expenses.

11.4. Building an Emergency Fund

Having an emergency fund gives you the freedom to endure life's unexpected turns, making it an essential step in your financial success path. Aim to have three to six months of living expenses in your emergency fund.

11.5. Reducing and Managing Debt

Being in debt drastically reduces your financial freedom. Paying interest on debt takes away money that you could be saving or investing. Therefore, another critical step in your financial journey is to reduce and manage your debt efficiently. Start with higher interest loans (usually credit cards) and gradually work on others.

11.6. Investing Your Money

Investing your money wisely can fast-track your financial success journey. Understand different investment options like bonds, stocks, mutual funds, real estate, and understand their risk-return trade-off. Never put all eggs in one basket; diversify your portfolio in line with your financial goals and risk tolerance.

11.7. Regular Financial Reviews

With a set plan, a budget, and investments in place, regularly reviewing your finances is the final piece of the puzzle. It ensures you stay on the right financial path and makes room for any adjustments needed due to changes in your financial goals, market performance, or personal circumstances.

Creating personal financial success is an ongoing process and not an overnight event. As life changes, so too do your financial circumstances, needs, and goals. It is, therefore, important to keep refining your strategies as you march along your path of financial success. By taking these steps, you will be able to control your financial future and create the unique path to financial success you desire.

Whether you are from a high-income bracket or hover around median income statistics, these principles and steps apply. They demand patience, discipline, and continued efforts but rest assured the end result will be worth it: financial success designed on your terms and adapted to your life.

www.ingramcontent.com/pod-product-compliance
Lightning Source LLC
Chambersburg PA
CBHW060854260726
48661CB00008B/3260